———— *SUCCESSFUL* ————

Piano Solos

*A new collection especially suitable
for teaching, recital and general use*

G. SCHIRMER, Inc.

DISTRIBUTED BY

7777 W. BLUEMOUND RD. P.O. BOX 13819 MILWAUKEE, WI 53213

ED. 2242

ALPHABETICAL INDEX BY TITLE

ALPHABETICAL INDEX BY COMPOSER

The Swan

From "The Carnival of Animals"

Camille Saint-Saëns
Arranged by Henry Levine

43957cx

4

Carnival of Venice

Italian popular melody
of the early 19th century
Arranged by Luis Jordá

Moderato

43957

Barcarolle
from "Contes d'Hoffmann"

Offenbach
Arr. by S. Camillo Engel

Knight Rupert*
from "Album for the Young"

Robert Schumann, Op. 68, No. 12

* There is no English equivalent for this legendary German character who, clad in a rough Santa-Claus costume, makes his rounds before Christmas and catechizes the children concerning their behavior.

Plaisir d'amour
Joy of Love

Giovanni Martini (1741-1816)
Arranged by Henry Levine

Andantino

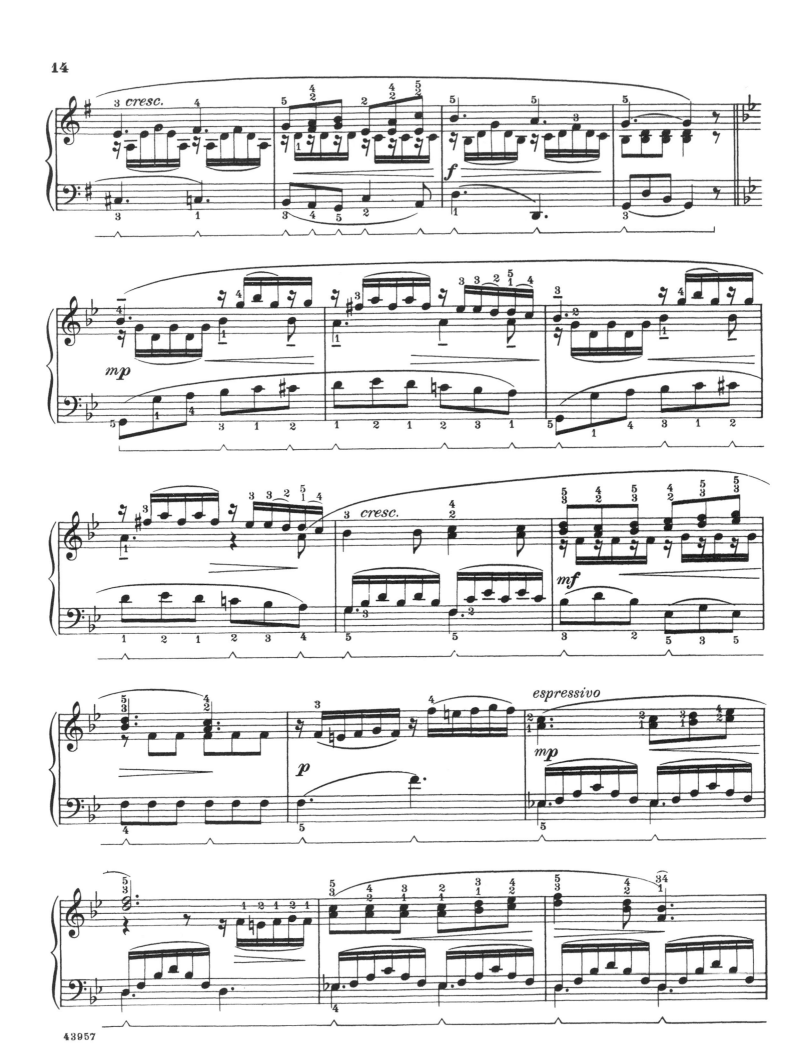

43957

The Stars and Stripes Forever

March

John Philip Sousa

Under the Double Eagle

March

J. F. Wagner, Op. 159

Trio.

D. C. al Fine.

Sonatina

Fingered and phrased by
LUDWIG KLEE.

Fr. Kuhlau, Op. 55, No. 1

*) Remark: These small slurs indicate that the last bass-note in one measure should be carefully connected with the first bass-note in the next.

43957

Song of the Lark

from "Album for the Young"

P. Tschaikowsky; Op. 39, No. 22

To a Wild Rose

from "Woodland Sketches"

Edward MacDowell, Op. 51 No. 1

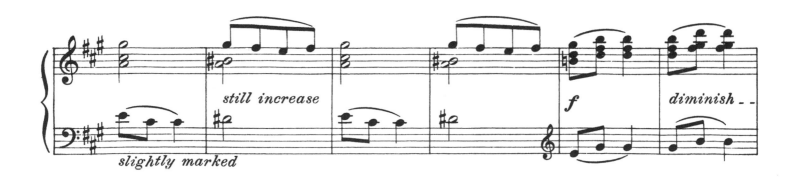

Poupée Valsante

Edited and fingered by
Louis Oesterle

Ed. Poldini

Opening Theme
from Piano Concerto No. 1

Peter Ilyitch Tchaikovsky, Op. 23
Arranged by Carl Deis

Andante non troppo e molto maestoso

43957

*These anticipatory chords may be omitted.

43957

Bagatelle

Andante grazioso, quasi Allegretto.(♩=56.)

L. van Beethoven, Op. 33, No. 1

a) With this sort of accompaniment the left hand must always be subordinate to the right.

b)

a) Less advanced players, who cannot immediately (or perhaps cannot at all) play those eight notes with equality over against the left hand eighth notes, may at first (or always) play thus:

b) The left hand part, containing the melody is to be emphasized.

c) The Bass note A♭ as well as the low E♭ in the next bar, must subordinate to the melody contained in the upper voice of the left hand part.

Six Easy Variations

on a

Swiss Song *)

Edited and fingered by
SIGMUND LEBERT

L. van Beethoven

*) We call special attention to these thoroughly de-lightful Variations because they are far too little known and appreciated. They will be particularly welcome to *young* pianists.
(a) By a comma we mark those points at which the player ought, by lifting his hands a little earlier than the note-value indicates, to bring out a rhythmical division.
(b) Proceed without interrupting the rhythm; and similarly after Variations 1 and 3.

43957

Minor

Poco sostenuto e doloroso (♩ = 112)

Var. III

sempre p e legato

Major

Tempo I un poco animato (♩ = 126)

Var. IV

legato

Ped. simile

Musetta's Waltz-Song

from "La Bohème"

Giacomo Puccini

Scotch Poem

Fern an schottischer Felsenküste,	Far away on the rock-coast of Scotland,
Wo das graue Schlösslein hinausragt	Where the old grey castle projecteth
Über die brandende See,	Over the wild raging sea,
Dort am hochgewölbten Fenster,	There at the lofty and archèd window,
Steht eine schöne, kranke Frau.	Standeth a woman beauteous, but ill,
Zartdurchsichtig und marmorblass,	Softly transparent and marble pale;
Und sie spielt die Harfe und singt,	And she's playing her harp and she's singing,
Und der Wind durchwühlt ihre langen Locken	And the wind through her long locks forceth its way,
Und trägt ihr dunkles Lied	And beareth her gloomy song
Über das weite, stürmende Meer.	Over the wide and tempest-toss'd sea.

Heinrich Heine

Edward MacDowell. Op. 31, № 2

Allegro tempestoso

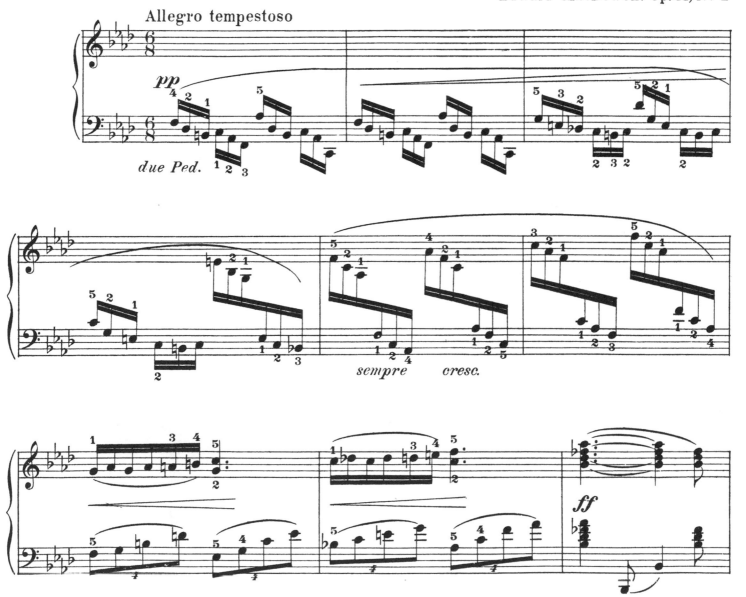

If I could tell you

Idabelle Firestone
Arranged by Henry Levine

Andante moderato, con espressione

Whispering Hope

Alice Hawthorne
Arranged by Charles Dews

43957

War March of the Priests

from "Athalia"

Felix Mendelssohn
Arranged by E. Pauer

Étude
A Glee

Rudolf Friml. Op. 85 bis, No. 5

43957

Notturno

Edited and fingered by
Louis Oesterle.

Edvard Grieg, Op. 54, No. 4

43957

To Mrs. Helen M. Scoville, New York City.

Arabian Night.
Romance for Piano.

Albert Mildenberg.

43957

Plaintively, and a trifle faster

Menuet

Edited and fingered by
L. Vollmer

I. J. Paderewski. Op. 14. № 1

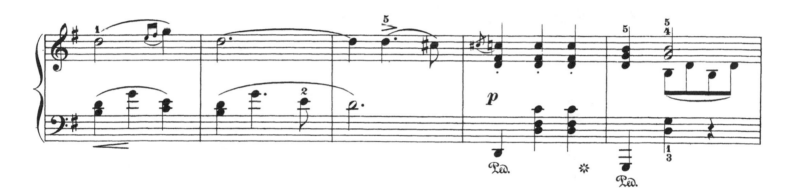

Pastorale

Edited and fingered by
G. Buonamici

Domenico Scarlatti
Arranged by Carl Tausig

43957

Oh Promise Me

Reginald de Koven
Transcribed for Piano by James H. Rogers

Wedding March

from "Lohengrin"

Richard Wagner
Arranged by E. Pauer

Poco piu lento.

Tempo I.

Impromptu

F. Schubert, Op. 142, No. 2

43957

Hallelujah! from "The Messiah"

G. F. Handel

Allegretto moderato.

Valse

Edited by Carl Deis

Auguste Durand, Op. 33

43957

Seconde Valse Brillante

Revised and fingered by
Wm Scharfenberg.

Benjamin Godard. Op. 56.

Arioso

Johann Sebastian Bach
Transcribed for Piano Solo by
Max Pirani

43957

Papillon

(Butterfly)

Revised and fingered by
Wm Scharfenberg.

Allegro grazioso.(♩ = 132.)

Edvard Grieg, Op. 43, No. 1

Sabre Dance

From "Gayne" Ballet

Aram Khachaturian
Arranged by Henry Levine

Whims
(Grillen)
from "Fantasiestucke"

Robert Schumann, Op. 12, No. 4

43957

43957

Fantasia I in D Minor

Revised, phrased, and fingered by
Giuseppe Buonamici

W. A. Mozart

43957

Fantaisie-Impromptu

Revised, edited and fingered by
Rafael Joseffy

F. Chopin, Op. 66, No. 4
Posthumous

Allegro agitato

43957

Étude

Revised and fingered by
Arthur Friedheim

F. Chopin, Op. 10, No. 3

Lento ma non troppo (♪ = 69)

43957

Intermezzo

Revised and edited by
Carl Deis

Johannes Brahms, Op. 119, No. 3

Grazioso e giocoso

43957

Arabesque No. 1

Claude Debussy

Tempo rubato (*un peu moins vite*)

Prélude

Specially edited by
The Composer

Serge Prokofieff. Op. 12, No. 7
1913

Vivo e delicato (♩ = 138)

43957

Impromptu.

Edited and fingered by
Louis Oesterle.

Hugo Reinhold, Op. 28, No. 3

Allegro molto possibile.

Copyright, 1898, by G. Schirmer, Inc.
Copyright renewal assigned, 1926, to G. Schirmer, Inc.

Tempo I.